FOUND:
Rediscovering Your Dreams, Your Voice, and Your Life in 15 Minutes a Day

LAIN EHMANN

Copyright © 2015 Lain Ehmann
All rights reserved. No part of this publication may be reproduced, distributed, or transmitted in any form or by any means, including photocopying, recording, or other electronic or mechanical methods, without the prior written permission of the publisher, except in the case of brief quotations embodied in reviews and certain other non-commercial uses permitted by copyright law.

DEDICATION

For my coaching clients, especially those in Living Life Loud, ROAR!, and the No-Bummer Summer. You all inspire me every day with your determination to take life on your terms.
I love you!

TABLE OF CONTENTS

DEDICATION iii
INTRODUCTION vii
CHAPTER 1: THE BACKGROUND 1
CHAPTER 2: WHAT THE HECK IS AUTHENTICITY
  (AND WHY SHOULD I CARE)? 7
CHAPTER 3: WHAT AUTHENTICITY IS – AND ISN'T 11
CHAPTER 4: HATERS GONNA HATE 15
CHAPTER 5: HOW AUTHENTICITY HELPS US WITH OUR
  LIFE'S MISSION 19
CHAPTER 6: WHAT IF...? 23
CHAPTER 7: VALUING YOU 27
CHAPTER 8: WHEN BAD THINGS HAPPEN TO
  GOOD PEOPLE 31
CHAPTER 9: HOW TO (REALLY) CHANGE YOUR LIFE 37
CHAPTER 10: A WORD ABOUT FEAR 41
CHAPTER 11: JUST THE BEGINNING 47
CHAPTER 12: FAQs 49
CHAPTER 13: YOUR ACTION PLAN 59
RESOURCES 61
YOUR INVITATION 63
ABOUT THE AUTHOR 65

INTRODUCTION

Do you have laryngitis of the soul? Do you feel like your voice – who you really are without all the roles of mother, sister, daughter, wife, friend – is silent, or is such a tiny little whisper that you can barely even hear it under the cacophony of other people's voices and demands?

If so, you aren't alone. Most women I work with tell me that they have lost their voice, lost their dreams, lost themselves, after years of living for other people. But there's still something inside of them longing to be heard. They want to live life louder, without having to conform to the expectations of other people's dreams, goals, and priorities. Somehow they woke up and found themselves in a life they didn't realize they were creating, and something in the pit of their stomach said that it may already be too late.

Maybe you want to start your own cupcake business, or get your law degree, or run for the school board, or write a blog, or take a coding class, or apply for a new job. Maybe you want to lose 20 pounds, or dye your hair red, or start wearing funky necklaces and swirly skirts. Or maybe you're not sure WHAT you want, but you know there's something in you that is beating on the doors of your heart, longing to be exposed. But you're scared.

You're scared because you haven't let that side of yourself out for years – maybe not ever.you've always kept it locked up. You know there's more to you than mom, wife, daughter. and daughterBut those roles are so heavy and take so much time that there's not much room left for you when the day is done. So you continue on, pushing your dreams to the side, letting other people take center stage, because it's easier that way. And then one day you wake up and you ask, "Is this all there is?"

The answer is, NO. There is more. You can have more. You are worth more. And I want to help you get it. Whatever your dreams, I truly believe that you are not only entitled to them, but the world needs you to make them into a reality. Our society is in a troubled place. We need miracle-makers and dreamers. We need YOU.

But first, you have to figure out what it is you really want. You have to figure out who you are at the core, after the other stuff has been peeled away. And that's what authenticity is all about: Defining you and your life on your own terms. It's not an easy process, but it is a simple one, and that's what this book is all about. In its pages, I will lead you on a process of finding out what that little voice is really saying, and in the process of listening, you just might find the secret to the life of your dreams.

Over the years I've led dozens of women through the process of excavating themselves from the piles of laundry, expectations, and roles they've found themselves buried in. As an author, speaker, and business/life coach, I've helped women start businesses, redefine relationships, and recreate their lives into something they adore. And I can help you too. I am an expert at leading women back to themselves, no matter how lost they've gotten. It all starts with claiming yourself.

Imagine living each day on your terms, knowing without a doubt that you are doing the work you were meant to do, with the people

FOUND

who set your soul on fire. Imagine letting go of the expectations, roles, and responsibilities that feel more like boulders around your neck than symbols of success. Imagine feeling light, free, and excited about each day. That kind of life is your birthright, and I can help you get it, if you're willing to do the work.

One of my coaching clients, Gina, said, "Working with you has been an amazing experience and I have grown SO MUCH. I have a different set of coping skills that focus more on me and what I need rather than how others perceive me and what they think. At the end of the day, I just have myself to be accountable to - not the outside world... Sometimes it takes one person to change my perspective and I'm so grateful that you have helped me create a new and improved me."

Another client, a mom of two, said, "I am glad to have reaffirmed that my values are important to me. This is where I find my authentic self... I am learning that I like who I am and that being honest with myself is the most important thing that I can do."

If you are ready to start living louder...

...If you're ready to take up space in your own world...

...If you're ready to stop settling for what life gives you and ask for what you truly want...

I can help you! In just a few short hours you can be on your way to living a life more colorful, more passionate, and more exciting than you ever dreamed possible. I'm not going to make you attend a month-long yoga retreat and eat wheatgrass and tofu, or ask you to toss out your kids and the dog and move to a commune where you weave flax and hemp wall hangings, or to chant or burn incense or pray to your spirit guides. Instead, the process is very practical, and the changes will be mostly internal. The path you will take is as individual as you are, and you only have to do what feels right to you. Give me a week, and I'll lead you on the most exciting journey of your life: The journey back to YOU.

You might be saying that you don't have the time right now because you have all those Girl Scout cookies to sort and deliver. Or maybe your son is graduating next month, or there's a big work project that needs to be finished, or you want to wrap up binge-watching the last season of *Mad Men* before you commit to anything. That's fine – but please realize what's at risk. Each day you delay, each week you put off finding out what you really want, is a day or week or month or year you've squandered on someone else's priorities, someone else's dreams, someone else's passions.

Something prompted you to pick up this book to begin with. That little voice won't yell or scream or throw a temper tantrum to make you listen. Instead, it will just go back to its corner and silence itself, until one day you can't hear it anymore.

Isn't it time you paid attention?

CHAPTER 1

THE BACKGROUND

"Get real."

"Be yourself."

"Show the real 'you.'"

"Honesty sells."

"Live your truth."

You've heard all the quotes, advice, and pithy suggestions about the latest buzz word, authenticity. It all sounds good and strikes a chord deep within. But when it comes to defining exactly what authenticity is and how you can use it to your advantage in your personal and professional life, things get tough.

- Does authenticity mean sharing all your innermost feelings on Facebook, sharing with the world every nuance of your life from having horrible PMS to getting in a fight with your mother?

- Does it mean speaking up every time someone says or does something you disagree with, whether it's the dude in front of you in line at CVS or the mom sitting next to you in the bleachers at the softball game?

- Does it mean refusing to bend to the cultural norms that say what it is you can and can't do, and letting your crazy fly high and wide?

- Does it mean letting go of responsibilities and relationships that "cramp your style" and roaming free?

- And what the heck do you do if you don't have the slightest idea what "your truth" is?

As a child and young adult, I had no sense of what it meant to listen to my own voice. I grew up as "the good girl," driven to make others happy and keep the peace in an often tumultuous household. I didn't know what I wanted except to be as perfect as possible so everyone around me would be happy and stay calm. As a result, when I hit adulthood, I had no idea what I wanted. I'd always done what others wanted and couldn't even begin to figure out where I fit in.

It took me a long time to find my way back to myself. I read hundreds of books, went to counseling, worked with a life coach, journaled, went to seminars, researched, and even became trained as a personal and life coach myself. After a lot of effort, successes – and failures! – I have a good sense of who I am. Whether people read my books, hear my audios, watch me on video, or meet me in person, my goal is that they feel they know me – that I'm the same in one medium as I am in another.

I've spent most of my adult life trying to figure out what it means to live an authentic life, and I've done so with more success at some times than at others. The one thing I know for sure is that becoming authentic

FOUND

is a PROCESS, one that looks different for each one of us. And while I'm in complete support of figuring out your unique take on the world, I do suggest doing so while paying attention to personal hygiene. Being "real" doesn't have to mean looking (and smelling) like the bride of Grizzly Adams, or quitting your 9-to-5 just because you feel like you have to.

In fact, living an authentic life is more about awareness than it is about any particular behavior. There are times, for instance, that someone close to me says something that I am diametrically opposed to – for instance, that Starbucks coffee is totally better than Dunkin' Donuts – and I choose to let it go. Because of the situation, the size of the hurt, or the perceived intent of the comment, I may let it wash over me like a wave of slightly smelly yet ultimately harmless water. I'm not denying my feelings or caving to external pressure; I'm making an informed decision to allow something to pass by.

It's like being in a crowded supermarket (do you see how so many of my examples have to do with retail therapy? Yeah, I noticed that too…). Someone rams into your bupkus on aisle 4, just as you were bending down to get a container of Chobani. Incensed, you turn around and notice that the guilty party, an octogenarian wearing a muu-muu and Jackie O sunglasses, can barely see over her cart, heaped as it is with Feline Friskies and extra-large size bottles of prune juice. Do you grab her by her scrawny throat, throw her up against the side of the cooler, and threaten her with death by a thousand reruns of "Golden Girls" if she ever dares to touch your booty again? Or do you give her a raised eyebrow (that she probably doesn't see) and go on about your day?

I certainly hope you went with Option B. Because if you make it a regular habit to accost every little old lady who dares to step on your foot, cut in front of you in line, or otherwise invade your personal space, you're wasting a lot of energy – energy that could be better spent on the important things in life, like alphabetizing your spice rack or trimming your gerbil's cuticles.

By choosing to overlook this perceived slight, you aren't being inauthentic or fake. You're not demeaning yourself or saying that you don't deserve "respect." Instead, you are making decisions based on your personal values and choosing to focus on the more important stuff.

To me, that's what authenticity is – knowing who you are and what is important to you, and having a core that doesn't change, no matter what the situation. It means coming to life with a quiet strength born of an inner knowledge. And when you have that knowledge and strength, you don't have to flex your muscles all the time. You know who you are, so it doesn't matter if someone else has a different opinion. It truly just slides right past you, and your life is better as a result.

That's what we're going to be discussing – how to make our lives better. This book is not intended as a substitute for therapy (in fact, if you find yourself regularly grabbing old ladies in the supermarket, you just might want to contact a mental health professional and investigate some anger management treatment). It is, however, intended to give you practical and actionable information and advice as to how you can begin living in accordance with your values, how you can handle blow-back from others who don't see the world quite the same way you do and wish you'd just go back to being a wimpy suffer-in-silence type, and how your

FOUND

world will start to change for the better when you start figuring out what exactly you're here to do – and not do.

Through my own exploration, training, education and research, I've discovered some great stuff on the topic of authenticity that I'm excited to share with you. I've already shared a lot of this information with my coaching clients and audience through my classes, speaking, videos, blog posts, and more, and I'm excited to pass it on to you as well.

If you're ready to start living your life a little louder, with a little more clarity, energy, and excitement, then let's get this show on the road. After all, time, tide, and the Nordstrom half-yearly sale wait for no woman.

CHAPTER 2

WHAT THE HECK IS AUTHENTICITY (AND WHY SHOULD I CARE)?

I knew since I could talk that I wanted to be a writer. I wrote little stories and poems all through my childhood. I was an editor for three years on the school paper. But when it came time to declare my major in college, my mom told me not to do journalism. "Journalism is no job for a woman," she told me. "You have to move around and you don't get paid anything. You could never be a mother and be a journalist."

I believed her. And so I went to college and grad school, pursuing a "safe" career in public administration. While there were parts I enjoyed, I was still writing on my own, never imagining that it could be a career because "women couldn't do that."

I like to believe my mom had my best interest at heart. She wanted me to have a secure future, doing something with job security. And she's right – government is pretty secure. But for me, it was also mind-numbing. I spent a year in this "safe" job, crying every single day, hating my life, wishing I was somewhere and someone else. From the outside, it probably looked pretty good: I was getting paid pretty well, my position was kind of prestigious, and I got to wear heels to work. But I despised it. I sat at my desk feeling like, at age 23, my life was being sucked out of me, spreadsheet by spreadsheet.

It took me a long time to work myself back to my dreams, a step at a time, first working in PR because I wanted to "write more," then working in marketing communication, then finally – FINALLY – declaring myself a freelance journalist. And I loved it. Writing was what I was meant to do, and it hardly ever feels like work. Iit's like a dolphin cutting easily through the saltwater; sometimes it's tough, but it's home.

It took me a detour of about 10 years, two degrees spanning five years at universities on both coasts, and hours and hours of counseling before I found my way back. Sometimes I bemoan all those lost years (Who would I be if I had actually pursued the path of my dreams a decade earlier? What could I have created by now?). But that's water under the bridge. I want to use my experience to help you bypass the detour and get on track NOW. I want you to live the life you always dreamed of, fulfilling the goals I know you can reach.

And the first step of that is learning how to be authentic and declaring what it is you really want.

Have you ever seen someone so comfortable in his or her own skin that they radiate confidence and positive energy like one big ole' ball of happy juice? They're not necessarily the most handsome, beautiful, talented, or charismatic person in the room. But because they have such an unwavering sense of who they are, you can't help but pay attention. Lady Gaga, Donald Trump, Oprah Winfrey, Charles Barclay – love 'em or hate 'em, they know who they are and what they have to offer.

As a result, their feet seem so grounded. They are planted, like nothing will throw them off, as if the rest of the world needs to bend to their will

FOUND

instead of vice-versa. They are powerful, free, certain, and strong – and more attractive because of their strength. They could do anything. They are superheroes.

That sense of self comes from, in part, knowing that some people are going to love you and some people are going to hate you, and there's not a lot you can do to sway them in either direction. With that knowledge comes a freedom – a freedom to do what you want, say what you want, and be who you want, in accordance with your own values. Heck, if people are going to be mad at you whether you vote for Team Sharks or Team Jets, you may as well go with your heart, right? At least you're sure of making ONE person happy.

So often, though, we base the decisions for our life – Should I go to law school? Should I cut my hair short? Should I take Job A or Job B? – on what we think other people will say, want, or judge. We are so scared of others' opinions that some of us spend our whole lives trying to bend ourselves to other people's wills. Our mom wanted us to skip medical school to get married, so we did. Our husband wanted us to stay home with the kids, so we did. The kids wanted us to be at every soccer game, every play rehearsal, every playdate, so we did. The other moms wanted us to fit in and look a certain way, so we did.

It can get so bad that we don't even recognize ourselves anymore. What happened to the little girl who wanted to fly planes like Amelia Earhart, or be a Supreme Court Justice, or join the circus? She became buried under a landslide of other people's expectations, opinions, and judgments. It's time to dig her out.

CHAPTER 3

WHAT AUTHENTICITY IS – AND ISN'T

I had a person in my life – let's call her "Mom," because that was her name – who was pretty critical. I mean, mega-critical. If she hadn't come up with the idea or pre-approved the plan, it was wrong, plain and simple. And she made no bones about telling you.

If I ever mentioned that her critical words stung, she'd say, "Well, that's just the way I am. I guess you don't want me to be honest." As a kid, I didn't know how to handle this. Of course I wanted her to tell me the truth, but I also didn't want her to be cruel. I didn't know there was a third option, so I kept my mouth shut and accepted her unwarranted, never-ending stream of criticism. I tried to bend my life to fit her judgment, because after all, she was my mom. She knew best, right?

Now that I'm older and way wiser, I know that she didn't know best and that her negativity was a sign of her own insecurity. She attempted to cloak cruelty in "honesty" so it would be more acceptable. But it wasn't. It isn't. Authentic people don't attempt to bring others down so they can feel better about themselves. Authenticity comes from your heart and soul, so as a result, it is never cruel.

Being authentic doesn't mean you always speak your mind. Some people use "keeping it real" as an excuse to be rude and blunt, but that's not necessary. You're not betraying your innermost soul if you refrain from telling your cousin that her new haircut looks like it was done by a blind three-year-old with safety scissors. If you choose to let that opinion fly, you're just being mean, not authentic.

Being authentic doesn't mean you insult others and walk all over the rest of the world. You can be kind, and compassionate, AND stick to your beliefs, making your decision and moving forward, without changing your position based on external pressure. If you don't like racial slurs, then you don't like them, no matter who is dishing them out; your preference doesn't change based on the fact that the one hurling the insults is considered "cool" or is in a position of power.

Imagine having that kind of inner strength – to chart your own course without worrying about what others outside your closest advisors will think or say. That would be pretty darned awesome. No second-guessing. No wondering if you should or shouldn't have spoken up. No worrying about "the optics" or the blowback from bystanders. You just keep on keeping on, knowing you're always going to be okay, and that you are as entitled to your opinions as the next person.

Most of us are just the opposite. We worry from the moment we get up until the moment we go to bed. What will the kids at school think of the zit on your nose? What will the people in the office think of the new car you just got? What will your mother, father, sister, uncle, next-door neighbor, Facebook friend think of your decision to stay home with your kids/go back to work/bottle feed/breastfeed/go back to school/drop out of school?

FOUND

It's exhausting! Contrast that never-ending chatter in the back of your brain with the quiet confidence that those who are operating from their deepest values – their core – enjoy. It's the difference between trying to tune in an AM radio show in the middle of the Mojave Desert and having SiriusXM at your beck and call 24/7.

When you have that sense of self, you also engender more trust from others. They know who you are and what you stand for, and they know you're going to be consistent, regardless of the situation or which way the winds blow. That level of trust brings new opportunities and relationships, ones that wouldn't come to you if you were Mr. or Ms. Wishy-Washy.

Right about now, you may be getting mad. Some of that anger is directed at yourself. You feel like you've been living halfway, hiding behind the mask of "good daughter" or "good wife" or "good friend." You're pissed off because you've sold out on yourself. You know you're worth more. That anger is good! It's empowering. It means there is a part of you that is alive and screaming out to be heard. LET HER ROAR! We're going to channel that energy into positive forward motion.

Some of that anger also might be directed at the people in your life who you feel "did" this to you. Your parents, your old boyfriend, your teachers... they forced you into these roles that you despise and that are crushing your very soul. You may want to pick up the phone right now and yell at them, accusing them of abusing you, emotionally stunting you, wrecking your life.

If that's you, I have one piece of advice: Set the phone down.

It's natural to want to lash out and blame someone else for where you are. As I have processed my own story over the past years, I've had a lot of anger for a lot of people in my life. But blowing up at others in anger never works. It's like throwing a rock through a plate-glass window: It feels good in the split second as you let the stone fly, but then you see the destruction and are now dealing with a heck of a clean-up job. Blaming others is never helpful. There may come a time when you want to have some pointed conversations with others in your life, but those discussions need to come from a position of strength. Blaming others is saying you are weak, a victim, someone who couldn't take care of herself. And what we're doing here is the opposite of that. We're taking control, and that starts with owning where you are, right now.

CHAPTER 4

HATERS GONNA HATE

It would be awesome if being authentic ensured that we would be universally loved and/or admired, that any decision made from our heart would be "perfect." Unfortunately, that's not true. In fact, the more you direct your own life, the more you open yourself up to others' wrath and negative opinions. You stand out when you chart your own course, and there are a lot of people in the world who just don't like that.

You've seen it; after all, it's the subject of just about every John Hughes film. Do what you want and people will fight, pick on you, abuse you as they try to force you to comply. But these stories also show that if you're able to walk through the fire, you'll be rewarded on the other side. The good thing is, when you're doing YOUR thing rather than theirs, you have peace in the knowledge that you're walking the right path.

Remember that scene in *Pretty in Pink* when Molly Ringwald struts into the high school prom in her homemade funky dress, head held high, with the Duckman, played by John Cryer, at her side? If you haven't watched the movie, you need to drop everything and go watch it RIGHT. NOW. I'll wait.

Okay, wasn't that awesome? Not everyone loved her dress (it's actually pretty awful). Not everyone liked her. But it didn't matter. Once she was true to herself, she was okay. And that is the safety and power that authenticity gives you. You know where you stand, and the ground is firm under your feet.

If you believe in a higher power – and I certainly do! – you might even think that you're being given a trial run for bigger responsibility. If you can't handle it when the moms at your kids' school criticize you for not getting on the bandwagon to support the removal of peanuts from the school cafeteria, then how are you going to maintain your equanimity when your blog hits the big time and you start getting flamed by people you don't even know?

A few years ago, I wrote a satirical essay on the high cost of music lessons for a parenting website. In the piece, I made some offhanded comments about music teachers being unemployed musicians. Yeah, I know... it wasn't very nice, and in retrospect, I'd certainly form my statements a little more thoughtfully. After the initial piece had been posted, there was a bit of an uproar, but it soon died down. But little did I know that thanks to one of the vagaries of the Internet, that essay would come back to bite me a decade later and I would become persona non gratis to the entire piano teacher underground.

Somehow, a popular musician re-discovered that essay and linked to it, encouraging his readers to "let me have it." For about a week, I woke up every day to an inbox full of insults, comments on my parenting, and yes, even death threats. It was crazy! And there was a temptation to lash out at these angry music teachers, letting them know how childish they were being, or posting their names on my Facebook page so no one would ever hire them to teach music to little children again. But instead, I did nothing. Not. One. Thing.

The two people who did email me and calmly and politely took issue with my statements, I responded to. I admitted that my essay had been too cavalier, and I thanked them for their input. One even became a dear friend! But the others? I didn't even waste my time on them, nor did I spend a lot of time second-guessing whether I should have written what I wrote.

Was it tough? Definitely. Did I feel a pull to defend myself? For sure. Did I share my angst with my husband and close friends? Of course, I'm only human! But not for a moment did I consider asking the site to remove that essay. Right or wrong, these attackers were attempting to bully me into submission, and I refused to bow to their demands. I hold a core belief that we have a right to express our opinions, right or wrong, and no one should attempt to silence us. In this case, authenticity meant standing out there in the public eye as rotten tomatoes were thrown at me. Did I like it? No way. But I do know it made me a stronger person. Not only did I hold my course, I showed my kids that we can do tough things even when it seems that everyone is against us. And I showed the Universe that I'm ready for the big time.

CHAPTER 5

HOW AUTHENTICITY HELPS US WITH OUR LIFE'S MISSION

Another question many of us have is, "What's my life purpose?" We wonder why we're here, and what we're supposed to accomplish. If we're changing direction every time a celebrity we admire espouses a new fad, or the person we're dating picks up a new interest and wants us to go along, it can be nearly impossible to figure out who we really are and what we're gifted to do. When you understand who you are at your core, you can more easily sort through options, ideas, offers, and opportunities in order to select the ones that more accurately reflect your skills, goals, and values. This discernment keeps you from overbooking and overextending yourself in areas that aren't within your interests or desires.

One of my coaching clients had been a "yes girl" for years. She said yes to every request for help – from being the school library coordinator to the church potluck supper organizer to her kids' soccer team snack mom. If it needed to be done, people knew to ask Susan because she never said no. People would even ask her to help out at the elementary school even though her kids no longer attended! While she enjoyed being needed and got a certain level of reward from being that go-to gal, after working with me she realized that her heart wasn't in these activities. What she really wanted was to work on a few select volunteer opportunities and then build her own business. Her dream was to be an entrepreneur, not the Volunteer of the Year.

Saying "No" to all the people who had counted on her for so long was difficult. She heard lots of pleading and begging... "No one can do this but you." "You're perfect for this job!" "I was counting on you." But when she stuck to her guns, a funny thing happened: She WASN'T the only one who could chair the library book drive, or run the mission campaign, or drive carpool every morning. Other people stepped up and she was able to spend her time on the things that mattered most.

If she'd kept on hosting the foreign exchange students and volunteering as library coordinator and setting up the chairs before every school meeting, she never would have had the time to start HER business, write HER blog, get HER message out into the world.

There's a great quote that says, "You either work to build your dream, or you'll find yourself working to build someone else's." If you don't want to be a bit-player in your own life, if you don't want to lie on your deathbed wondering where all the time went, you need to draw a line. You can't do everything, and your stuff needs to get to the top of the list.

If you're a businessperson or business owner, all this goes double. People want to do business with those they trust and can count on. When they see you know who you are and can convey that, you have a leg up. But if you are changing your position on everything from the Red Sox to the color of your website header based on other people's input, no one is going to trust you. You've proven that you don't even know who you are, so why should they trust you with their hard-earned money? Who knows if you'll even be in business next week!

I don't mean to imply that once you start living from your place of authenticity, everything falls into place easily and effortlessly. As I shared earlier, it took me about ten years to get back to myself, and I still work on it. It's a daily practice as I continue to grow and circumstances in my life change. I've also had to fight some tough battles along the way. But the difference is that I know I'm fighting for my life, for what I think is right, not for someone else. I don't have to question my motives or whether it's "worth it." I know without a doubt that it is.

Now, I am in charge of my life, and I'm living it with a passion and freedom that would have seemed impossible a decade or two ago. I still get my heart broken by friends who don't love me the way I want them to, I still ache when my kids hurt and I can't help them, and I still get in arguments with my husband over who gets to control the TV remote (he always wins). But it's all the superficial stuff. I know that below the waves of the surface, I'm there. And I am strong enough to make it through. I will not be broken.

If that sense of certainty, comfort, and ease is something you long for, read on. No matter where you're starting from, you can become more authentic in your life, peeling back the layers that have kept the "real you" hidden from public view. Just imagine how amazing it will be to move through your life, feeling completely free and grounded. It's magical.

CHAPTER 6

WHAT IF...?

So I've sold you on the idea of living an authentic life, letting others see the inner you shine through. But the idea of peeling back those layers is daunting. Where do you start? What if other people don't like what they see? What if YOU don't like what you see?

That can be pretty scary. Some of my clients are worried they're going to strip away all the expectations and external pressures in their life, only to find that there's nothing left. "Who would I be if I wasn't a daughter, a friend, a mom?" they ask. "What will I do with myself if I'm not working towards the 'Volunteer of the Year' award?"

It's a good question. If you haven't been actively feeding your soul and your interests, you might find that you're a little rusty and stunted in that area. And there may be a period where you have to rediscover yourself, sitting with the emptiness.

There are two ways to enter into that space: One, you can see it as utterly terrifying and uncomfortable, so you rush to fill the empty slots in your calendar and in your life. You quit the quilting group you joined to make your mom happy, only to sign up for a hydroponic gardening class your husband is begging you to attend with him. You step down as church elder, only to get roped into being Sunday School organizer. The blank spots in your calendar are so scary that you throw anything into them, just to keep from sitting with yourself. Soon you find yourself back where you started, except now you're mad at ME: "This stuff doesn't work," you cry as you stuff envelopes and deliver Girl Scout cookies. "Lain has no idea what she's talking about."

Or you get really, really sick. Breaking a leg is not uncommon, nor is severe pneumonia or sinus infections or allergies. Or you have panic attacks where you feel, quite literally, like you are having a heart attack. Your body can't stand the thought of quiet, of calm, of NOTHING, so it decides it's a great time to shut down or overload. Don't laugh – it happens!

The other option sounds a little better: You see this process as a grand experiment, one to be relished and enjoyed. "Wow!" you say as you look at your blank planner. "I have NOTHING to do today! I think I'll go for a walk." Or take a nap. Or go to the library. Or meditate. Or paint. The discomfort is a sign of growth, an omen that you are on the right path, rather than a signal that you are dying.

You have the choice of which path to choose. You will likely feel discomfort when the phone doesn't ring and you don't have anything to do on a Tuesday night that used to be taken up with helping your friend pack orders for her vermiculture business. But then you breathe through it. You write about it. You explore. You CREATE something that comes from inside you. And then those crazy thoughts and worries about being bored for the rest of your life will disappear, bit by bit. In its place will be a new, beautiful, shiny life that you created from your own heart and soul.

FOUND

It's like going to a closet filled with hand-me-downs from someone a foot taller and 50 pounds heavier than you are and throwing everything out. At first, the emptiness is appalling. "What will I wear? Will I have to go naked? What have I done??" you'll ask. You have to refrain from running to Kohl's to assuage your fear by filling your cart with odds and ends, just so you have items hanging in your closet. If you give yourself a chance, you'll slowly fill the space with lovely clothes that fit you and your daily activities and that you feel great in. It may take some time to find the perfect pair of boots or just the right necklace, but by giving yourself the gift of patience, you'll be more pleased with the results.

And as for "other people," I guarantee that no matter who you are and what you do, there will be people who just don't like you. Maybe their first girlfriend who broke their heart into tiny smithereens had the same name. Or maybe they don't like your hair. Or your voice reminds them of the seventh-grade English teacher who used to mock their spelling paper in front of the entire class. It's going to happen, and you can't do a darned thing about it. So you can spend the rest of your life trying to please people who are never, ever going to like you. Or you can spend the rest of your life pleasing the only person you can reliably make happy – you.

I saw a poster the other day that summed this up perfectly: "I can only please one person a day. Today is not your day. Tomorrow isn't looking so good either."

A little snarky, yes, but oh-so-true. We CANNOT please anyone else on a long-term basis. We may be able to wear what they want us to wear or talk the way they want us to talk, but if we're acting a part, we're going to slip up at some point. And then when that happens either they're going to be mad that we were pretending or mad that we slipped up. It's a never-ending cycle. The only way out is to know ourselves, what we think, what we believe, and what's important to us, and act in accordance with that.

What if we don't like what we see? Typically, we end up despising ourselves when we feel we've sold ourselves out, giving in to get along, or sacrificing our values because we were too wimpy to stand up and proclaim our truth. While we may run into conflict when we speak and live our truth, I have never met someone who disliked the person they were becoming as a result of doing this inner work. In fact, quite the opposite. My clients realize how much they like that person who is willing to live according to her principles, regardless of the external consequences.

As far as where to start, that's the easy part. We start at the wellspring of all that is good and right – no, not Apple Corporate Headquarters in Cupertino, silly! We start with your values.

CHAPTER 7

VALUING YOU

Your values are, quite simply, the things that are most important to you. They are uniquely yours, and they may vary at different times in your life. What you valued as a five-year-old probably involved My PrettyLittle Pony and Care Bears, while what you want now hopefully has evolved quite a bit. Despite their ever-changing nature, values are wonderful snapshots of who you are, right here and now. And without knowing your values, it's impossible to live in accordance with your priorities.

In fact, you can't even have priorities because everything is decided externally. What is important is whoever is yelling loudest to get your attention. Imagine a hospital emergency room with 50 people in the waiting room. A few have gunshot wounds, four were in a bar brawl, a handful were involved in a car accident. There's a little kid who stuck a marble up his nose, an infant who sounds like she has an ear infection, and there's one old guy who just keeps shouting for Velma, whoever she is. Then there are a few sitting quietly, holding various parts of their bodies. If you were the intake nurse and had no process for evaluating the injuries, you would likely just run to whoever was yelling or screaming the loudest, whether that be the dude with the knitting needle sticking out of his thigh or the old guy looking for Velma.

As a result, some of the most important cases – the ones who are about to expire – would be overlooked, and you'd spend your time dispensing Tylenol and looking for Velma.

You have to stop leading your life based on public opinion, popular vote, or squeaky wheels. You need to have a list of priorities and marching orders you develop for your own life, that feed into the goals YOU want to accomplish today, tomorrow, next week, and next year.

If you are not clear on your values, you're living at the whims of the world, with no master plan. Think about a flag blowing in the wind. If the wind blows to the north, the flag flies in that direction. If the wind blows to the southeast, the flag flies that way. If it rains, the flag gets wet. If there's no wind, the flag just lies there like my Uncle Stewie after Thanksgiving dinner! A big, fat, nothing. (Sorry, Uncle Stewie!).

You are likely reading this book because you want more control in your life. You want to stop being treated like a lap dog, told when to come, when to sit, when to eat, when to go out. You want to be in charge, driving towards your destiny and all the bright, shiny fun your future holds, instead of being driven like a none-to-smart donkey with a load. You want to stand up and own your life, living it on your terms. Sounds good, doesn't it?

The first thing you need to grasp is the idea that your life, right now, is an outward manifestation of your values. What that means is that where you are now is a direct representation of your choices. And your choices are a reflection of your values. There is no way around it.

You could say, "Well, I didn't choose what I wanted to choose. I did it for my family." Well, then your family was a higher priority than your business goal, your fitness, your health, your art, whatever. Your life is PROOF of what you choose. Always.

You could say, "Well, I didn't CHOOSE to get in a car accident and end up disabled." That may be true, but you have chosen how you reacted to that accident. Some people become paraplegic and go on to change the world (Christopher Reeve for example). Others choose to give up and admit that life defeated them. The situation is the same; the only difference is the choice.

This can be a tough truth for some people. You want to say that something outside yourself is responsible for where your life is now... but the only one responsible for your life is YOU.

Let me say that again.

THE ONLY ONE RESPONSIBLE FOR YOUR LIFE IS YOU!

If you don't believe that, then you need to stop reading right now. There is no way you can move forward in your life, towards your goals, if you don't believe you are in charge of your life. The alternative is to hand your life over to others. While that might sound appealing in a way, it's basically abdicating your position as the sovereign power of your life. You're saying that others know what's best for you and your desires are worth less than theirs are. And that's just a bunch of BS.

You matter. Your dreams matter. Your goals matter. There are things on this earth for you to do that absolutely NO ONE else, none of the other 6-plus-billion humans on this planet, can do. And if you don't do them, they're not going to get done.

That might be a little scary to think about, but it's also incredibly empowering. You can look at all the other action items people have listed out in carefully bullet-pointed and color-coordinated lists and say, "Nope. That's not my job." And then you can get to your real work – the work of being you.

CHAPTER 8

WHEN BAD THINGS HAPPEN TO GOOD PEOPLE

With all this talk about personal responsibility and choice, you might think that I'm saying that bad things don't happen unless you invite them in. And who the heck would do that? I'm not saying that bad things don't happen. They do.

You have a miscarriage.

Your husband gets transferred to a new job out of state.

Your kid screws up in school.

Your mom gets sick.

Your dream company folds and you lose your job.

These things happen. In fact, every single one of them has happened to me! But each time, I chose to look for the positive. I chose strength. I chose to control what I could control. I chose to make the best of it. I chose NOT to be a victim. Every. Single. Time.

It wasn't always easy, but it was a choice. I remember standing in the office of my beautiful home in Monte Sereno, California, packing up my books because my husband had been transferred 3,000 miles away. We were leaving behind my family, my hometown, and a neighborhood and schools we adored. I turned to John and said, "I can't believe we're doing this."

He looked at me and answered, "Lainie, we could be packing up because we lost our house," as many had in the economic recession of the time. His words were like a bucket of cold water in my face, waking me up. We had a choice to look at that move as an adventure or as the worst thing that could have been visited upon us by an angry and vengeful universe. Right then, we made the decision to make the move the best thing that ever happened to our family – and it was. Was it what we would have chosen for ourselves? No, but it didn't matter. We chose the outcome.

A few years ago, I became unexpectedly pregnant. At age 44. With a kid about to enter high school. Good times. My husband and I were in shock, and then we got excited. This would be cool, we decided, even if it meant our kid would have to roll us in wheelchairs to his or her graduation. Babies are always a cause for celebration.

I put myself on bed rest due to my "advanced maternal age," I gave up Diet Coke, and then I started knitting. I made little blankets and a sweater and a hat or two. Because that's what people do when they're unexpectedly pregnant at 44, right?

And it was good. I lived on Lucky Charms and gained 10 pounds in three months and hit 13 weeks. My OB decided I was out of the woods except I wasn't and there was no heartbeat and my baby wasn't my baby anymore. And we cried.

FOUND

It was hard. It sucked for a while. It seemed like such a waste. But I made a choice – a choice that even this would not define me. It's part of my story, but I refused to allow it to become all of my story. I used it as a way to show my kids that bad things happen and we can handle them with grace and we can be miserable for a time, then we lift our heads up and keep moving forward. It doesn't mean we don't care or that we don't hurt. It does mean that we refuse to fall victim to the bad parts of life.

Everyone out there – EVERYONE – has stuff in their lives that has knocked them down. Maybe it's the death of a parent, or the death of a spouse, or the death of a dream or a child or an illness or betrayal or bankruptcy or life-altering accident. None of us get out of this life unscathed. But if you quit roller skating just because you fell down once and skinned your knee, what's the point?

When bad things happen, we need to refuse to let them be a waste. We need to find the meaning in them, the salvation, the silver lining, the hidden gift, even if we have to sort through all sorts of trash to discover it. Maybe we can use our story to help someone else, or maybe we learn something about ourselves or the way the world works. Or maybe it just makes a good cautionary tale (I am fairly certain that my kids have learned from my experience that birth control is NOT 100 percent effective!).

I've heard that life is 10 percent what happens to you and 90 percent how you handle what happens to you. So if you don't like what your life looks like, you need to take a good, hard look at your values and what you're choosing. I guarantee that somewhere on the path to your personal perdition, there was a choice you made that brought you to where you are right now. And even NOT choosing is a choice.

Many of us "go along to get along," letting other people set the course so we won't cause any conflict or rock the boat. They choose the vacation destination, the restaurant, the home, even our clothes, hobbies, and pastimes. My dad was so anti-conflict that every time we'd go out for dinner, he'd turn to my mom to ask her what he should order! If that sounds like you, it means the value being expressed is desire for lack of conflict, or harmony. Even if we spend every moment of our existence simply trying not to make waves, we are exhibiting our values. It means you value "lack of conflict" or "harmony" even at the expense of your own dreams and goals.

Remember: If you want to see what values you're living according to, just look at your life.

If you say you value financial security but you spend $500 you don't have on decorations to impress the moms at your kid's school, you value PRESTIGE or IMAGE more than financial security.

If you say you value your health but you constantly cancel your gym appointment because your mom calls for you to take her grocery shopping and you know she'll be mad if you tell her "No," you're prioritizing "lack of conflict" over your health.

So if you want to change your life, you need to start with an honest evaluation of where you are and how you got there. These are the steps:

1. **Figure out your values.** There are many free values assessments online. Take one or more of these tests, and then really look at the results. Are there any surprises? Where is your life out of joint

with your values? What are you going to do about it? *NOTE: If you'd like to access the free set of Authenticity Worksheets I've created to accompany this book, just go to www.lainehmann.com/freeauthenticityworksheets to download them. They make a great accompaniment to this book, and they'll lead you through the process of changing your life in only 15 minutes a day!*

2. **Figure out what you want from your life.** Be bold. The whole world is here for us to grab. Don't worry about what you "deserve" or are "entitled" to have. The universe is more concerned with what you will ask for, rather than what you'll settle for. If you'd like more information on dreaming big, check out my book on creating powerful vision boards to rock your future.

3. **Determine where you're already satisfied.** Even if there are big areas of improvement, there are likely some areas where you'd give yourself a pretty good grade. Name 'em and claim 'em! Success in one area can easily translate to success in another.

4. **Figure out where you're playing small or are disappointed in yourself.** Where do you constantly give up on your dreams? Where do you allow yourself to cop out with lousy excuses? Where do you know you could do better, but you just don't? We believe our own excuses far too often. If you are going to live an authentic life, it's time to stop listening to yourself.

Once you've gotten these four prompts answered – and it may take some time! – it's time to get to work. Roll up your sleeves, and get ready. Things are about to get real.

CHAPTER 9

HOW TO (REALLY) CHANGE YOUR LIFE

Maybe you already know what you want: To lose weight, get the house in shape, find a new job, a new mate, a new set of friends... That's terrific! It is possible to make improvements in your life just by sheer strength of will and iron determination. That's the way we're typically taught to do things. Want to lose weight? Restrict yourself to 1200 calories a day and run 10 miles a week and you should be good. Want to write a book? Commit to not getting up from your desk until you've penned 500 words each and every morning. And it works – to some extent.

But have you ever lost five or ten pounds, only to gain them back (and more!) when you returned to your old habits? If you're like me, you've lost 50 pounds... but unfortunately it's the same 5 pounds over and over again!

Have you scrimped and saved for months to build up a nest egg, only to blow the budget all in one fell swoop when you decided you just HAD to have a new TV?

Have you ever worked for weeks on your website, only to give it all up and never post a single blog post?

I remember signing up for a gym membership, getting all the

equipment for swim aerobics, and then never once stepping foot in the pool. Whoops.

If you can identify with any of these scenarios, you're not alone. That is because achieving long-term change is extremely difficult when we are trying to do it all on its own, through sheer force. We can make progress, but it's like trying to push a car that is in "park" with the emergency brake on. Uphill. It goes against the natural flow, so it's very, very hard.

I'm not saying that we can't change. We can! People do it every day. But they know that to make LASTING CHANGE, they must LINK THEIR GOALS to their HIGHEST VALUES. That means the goal is not set in isolation; instead, it's a reflection of their highest values and priorities. Just deciding to lose 20 lbs. is all well and good – but you're much more likely to actually lose the weight if there's a big "Why" behind it: An upcoming wedding, a high school reunion, a health diagnosis you want to avoid.

Here's an example: Think of a bad habit you have (biting your nails, smoking, drinking soda, whatever). If I told you to stop as of tomorrow, do you think you could do it? If you're like most people, you'd probably say, "Well, yeah. But why should I? Just because you say I should?"

And you'd be right. Why change something that is fulfilling on some level if you don't have a compelling reason to do so? That would be crazy. Why move yourself into the territory of discomfort if there's no payoff, no point, no end game? It's simply not worth the effort.

But what if I told you I'd pay you $1 million in cold, hard cash if you quit your bad habit for a month. Think your odds of completion would go up? You betcha! A lot of people would do it for a lot less than a cool $1 million. After all, we see people all the time putting themselves in crazy, unhealthy, dangerous, or embarrassing situations for a few grand, if that (it's called "reality TV").

And now, what if I told you that you'd be putting the lives of your entire family at risk if you continued with your bad habit? More likely than not, you've just smoked your last cigarette. The idea that your behavior is inextricably linked to the survival of someone you care about is enough for you to put the tobacco down, sometimes without a backward glance (This is exactly how I quit Diet Coke not once, but four times, for months on end).

The key wasn't the behavior; it was the desire behind the behavior. The more we can link the desired change to your highest values, the easier it is to change. By linking your soda consumption with your kids' lives, the choice becomes clear. I knew that my babies could be harmed if I drank caffeine and Aspartame while I was pregnant or breastfeeding, so it was easy for me to give it up. Since then, I've had trouble following through on my desire to re-quit, namely because there's no big "why." I know, I know – people say there are health benefits to quitting, but those are too removed from my experience to make them motivating (Don't judge).

Of course, not every decision is one of life and death. And no one is standing around, offering $1 million bonuses for getting to the gym every morning. But even at a less extreme level, linking our goals with our highest values helps us complete them. That's because when we don't live in accordance with our values, we experience discomfort caused by cognitive dissonance.

"Cognitive dissonance" is a fancy phrase that refers to the discomfort or unease that occurs when our outer world is at odds with our inner perceptions, or when we are trying to hold two conflicting beliefs or attitudes.

That means when there is a conflict between your behaviors and your beliefs, you get anxious, upset, uncomfortable, angry, depressed... Have you ever felt any of those? Yeah, I thought so. Me too. Maybe it happens when we tell ourselves we want to be a writer, yet we never manage to get more than a few pages into our book. Or maybe we think of ourselves as the thin, fit person of our youth – but when we look in the mirror, we see the results of years of poor diet and no exercise. Or maybe we like to claim that we are "good people" but we cheat on our taxes and lie to our spouses. These inner/outer conflicts feel horrible, so bad that we'll do almost anything to escape the discomfort and pain.

In fact, I think cognitive dissonance arising from a culture who's not living in accordance with its values is a leading cause of depression, obesity, and drug and alcohol abuse! We are not living according to our values, and so we feel uncomfortable. And then we try to do anything to get rid of that discomfort... anything except the hard work of living authentically. But you're not like that – at least, not anymore. You've seen what's in store for you, and you know how to make lasting change. It's pretty simple, actually.

CHAPTER 10

A WORD ABOUT FEAR

I lived most of my young life in a constant state of fear. I had a bowling ball I carried around in my stomach. It was so ever-present that I didn't know there was any other way to be or feel. I was constantly trying to please other people, to keep the peace, to keep our life on an even keel. As part of those efforts I got really good at doing what others wanted me to do.

I was the perfect student. The perfect daughter. The perfect girlfriend. And I hated it. I was always guessing what other people wanted from me, trying to balance the expectations from person A against person B. It was a no-win situation, and it burned me out. I spent most of my early 20's in an alternating state of depression and anxiety, crying almost daily. I was unbearably lonely, even in the midst of other people. After all, I couldn't let them see the real me. If they did, they'd leave me. My strategy was to try to please them all. And that often meant giving them way more of myself than I wanted to. But it was the only solution I knew. Soon there was nothing left.

When I finally took a stand for something I wanted, the blowback was tremendous. I told my parents I was moving to Boston after I graduated from grad school. I loved the city and knew no one – and that was just what I wanted and needed. My mom went ballistic. She told me she'd never feel the same about me again, that I was betraying her for not coming home to the Bay Area after finishing my master's degree. I did it anyway. It was the first time I had purposely done something against her wishes, and it was the scariest thing I had ever done. It was the beginning of my battle to reclaim myself.

Over the next 10 years, I dug myself out from the pile of expectations and rubble that I'd allowed to be piled upon me. It wasn't immediate. It was one small decision at a time, whether it meant standing up to the roommate whose unemployed boyfriend had basically moved into our small apartment, or deciding I wanted to leave a horrible job a year before my official commitment was up. I was fighting for my very survival. I knew if I didn't change, I would cease to exist. I chose to honor the small voice inside of me that told me there was more to me than "girlfriend," "daughter," and "employee." And I'm so glad I did.

It wasn't easy. It was terrifying. I suffered panic attacks, loneliness, and the slings and arrows of those who had been very used to me behaving in a certain way. But I survived, and I stand here on the other side to tell you how every bad moment, every disappointed friend or family member, every lost relationship, was totally worth it. Sure, I still miss those friends. I miss the closeness my mom and I had when I was basically her "mini-me," living the life she'd been unable to live. But what I have now – the freedom to be ME – is a treasure beyond rubies. I truly feel that I'm on the path to my life's purpose, the things that only I can bring to this world, the things that wouldn't exist if I hadn't chosen to fight for myself.

If you are shaking in your shoes right about now, you're not alone. Doing this kind of inner work requires determination and courage. It requires risk – and risk is never easy. You may very well make some people mad, and possibly even lose some friendships along the way. You may have a few sleepless nights, wondering why in the heck you listened to me in the first place.

I say that not to scare you, but to prepare you. Growth requires moving outside your comfort zone, and that, by definition, means making yourself deliberately uncomfortable in the hopes that someday in the future it will pay off.

It will. There will be days when you wish you could, in the words of *The Matrix*, go back and take the blue pill instead of the red. You'll wonder if the risk is worth the reward. You'll wonder what people will say when you push "publish" on the blog post, or tell your best friend a tough truth, or refuse to accept what's given to you and ask for more. You're going to be taking up more room in this world, and some people won't like that.

You may have to deal with some ugly comments or criticism. That's not fun. But what are you truly afraid of? Rejection?

What would you tell your son or daughter if they told you they were afraid of being themselves, for fear other people wouldn't like them? Most likely, you'd give them some variation on, "If they don't like you for who you are, they aren't worth your time." The same is true for you. If we have to go through life hiding who we are to gain approval, that's a pretty shoddy way to live (I was going to use another word beside "shoddy," but I want to keep this rated G!).

And here's the craziest part of this fairytale we've bought into: Hiding behind the mask doesn't keep us safe, either. It's like a little kid putting her hands over her eyes during a game of hide-and-seek. We think because we're putting up a bit of a smoke screen, they can't see us. But everyone sees right through the veneer. They know that what we're throwing up isn't the real us. It might look good at first glance, but there are cracks in the surface, and when any stress is applied, those cracks get bigger.

All it takes is financial, health, relationship, or parenting stress and things will break. The carefully curated life you created will crack wide open, letting the anger, jealousy, fear, envy, and anxiety out — and it might be the best thing that ever happened to you. Addicts in recovery will say that hitting rock bottom is what saved their lives because they had nothing left to lose. All their pride was stripped away, leaving only the broken shell of a human in need of help. And at our core, we're all broken. We all need help. We all need grace.

Living a fake life is what kills our soul. When we remove the masks we've worn for years upon years, we may lose some relationships. But the freedom we feel once we drop the pretense is worth it. All the effort we put into maintaining our aura of perfection or accommodation is now free to be applied to something that really matters. We weren't placed on this earth to stay small, to live lives of quiet desperation. We are here to roar, loud. And those who roar scare others. It makes them question their own small lives.

From everything we can tell, we get one go-round in this life. Use it to do something real, something true. It'll be worth it. I promise.

FOUND

NOTE: The two books that were most helpful with me in dealing with fear and daring are listed in the "Resources" section. Susan Jeffers' <u>Feel the Fear and Do It Anyway</u> helped me realize that fear truly is "<u>F</u>alse <u>E</u>vidence <u>A</u>ppearing <u>R</u>eal." And Brene' Brown's book, <u>Daring Greatly</u>, is a seminal work in the field of authenticity. Please read both.

CHAPTER 11

JUST THE BEGINNING

Living authentically means...

- figuring out our values
- saying no when we mean no
- having the tough conversations
- not shying away from conflict
- valuing ourselves as much as we value others

This is hard! Few people are able to take on this level of challenge in isolation. And that's why I have developed a group coaching program to assist people in living more authentic, powerful, REAL lives. If you think you might benefit from that kind of community, make sure to read the invitation at the end of this book.

Change is tough. Living authentically is tough. These are the battles we fight daily, but for which we rarely receive public acknowledgment. But make no doubt, the rewards do come. They come when we stand up for what we know to be right and true. They come when someone else sees us as an inspiration and feels empowered to speak their own truth. They come when we realize we are no longer a victim and we can take care of ourselves. They come when our daughters and sons look at us and say, "You are my hero."

So as hard as it is, it is possible. I've helped dozens of people change the way they live. And I'm here to help you, too.

This book is just the introduction to a life-long process. Living authentically isn't something that can occur in a day or even a year. It's something we choose over and over again, for as long as we live. While you've now seen some of the benefits to living an authentic life, you probably have some questions. I've put together an action plan that will lead you through the process of living an authentic life, in only 15 minutes a day. There's also an FAQ section to tackle some questions you might be having at this point.

CHAPTER 12

FAQs

1. **You say that I'm always living according to my values. So what's the problem? Sounds like I'm all set!**

Haha, you clever one. The problem is that we can live according to OLD values, UNEXAMINED values, or even SOMEONE ELSE'S values instead of INTENTIONAL values. I want you to examine the choices you're making to ensure you're headed in the direction you desire.

If you are living according to values someone else has foisted upon you, you're not living authentically. If you are living in accordance with values you may have created a decade or more ago, your life may not reflect the new you. We need to periodically check in with ourselves to see if we are headed in the direction we want for our lives.

Here's an example: In 2009 my family moved to Boston because of the job change I mentioned previously. The trip was amazing – exciting, educational, and fun – for about four years. And then the cold, the distance from what we considered "home," and the cost of living started wearing on us. What had been a great decision several years earlier no longer served us as our kids were getting older. So my husband and I decided to move to Arizona.

It wasn't something we'd anticipated. Our life plan never included "live in the Southwest." But at the time, we realized our priorities and values were no longer being met by the environment in which we lived.

Exercise: Right now, think of a decision you made in the moment that did not reflect your deepest values. Recall details of the situation. Who were you with? What did they say? What was the internal conflict you were dealing with? How did you feel after you made the decision?

2. Can my values change?

Sure! Just think about how some people totally change their lives when they have kids, or when they "hit rock bottom." If you've ever talked with someone who has had a diagnosis for a critical or fatal illness, they'll tell you that overnight things became very, very clear. They immediately knew what was worthwhile and what wasn't. The realigning of your values can happen in the blink of an eye.

When I was pregnant several years ago, I immediately adjusted my schedule. I knew that at my "advanced maternal age," I needed to take it much easier than I had with other pregnancies. Although technically my activities – Bikram yoga and running – were considered safe, and although the doctor didn't suggest I curtail my activities, I knew that I wanted to be absolutely sure I was giving this baby the best chance possible. So I quit yoga and exercise, cut way back on my work, and spent most of my day in bed. What had been important just a few weeks earlier – work, working out, etc. – was suddenly less important. BOOM.

My goal is to help you realign your life with your values without having to experience a life-threatening illness or other trauma. It is possible!

Exercise: Think of an example when your values changed in a split second. Maybe your child was at risk in some way. Maybe you got bad health news. What happened, and how did it affect your values?

3. I get this values thing, but I don't really see how it impacts my goal-setting.

As I stated in an earlier section, we can make changes in our lives through discipline or sheer will. But when we link our goals to our values, it becomes really simple. Knowing WHY we want to accomplish something is what grounds it in our hearts and in our soul.

This is a biggie, so let me give you an example.

Sara. Sara's stated values are family, building community, and helping others. Sara is $20,000 in credit card debt, largely because of a vacation she took last year with her family. One of her friends also was way behind on her rent and was going through a divorce, so Sara took out a cash advance and loaned her $5,000 which hasn't yet been paid back. She also regularly buys things for her kids and husband that they can't really afford, but she doesn't want them to feel deprived, so she charges it. And it's added up.

Now she is looking forward a few years to college for her kids, and she realizes they do not have anything saved. She wants to get debt-free, but is having trouble sticking to a budget and saying "no" to friends and family.

Once she realizes that her financial problems are directly impacting her family and her kids' ability to go to their desired colleges, it's easier for her to see WHY she needs to say "no" to a new pair of jeans or picking up the tab for friends who are strapped for cash when they go out for dinner. She's also been more assertive at work, and has volunteered for some extra projects so she can gain the skills necessary to get promoted and get a raise. Even though it's uncomfortable in the moment, she has her eye on her prize. Every time she has to put herself out there, she pictures her kids attending college, and she contrasts that with a picture of her kids' faces when she tells them they can't afford to send them to their dream school.

She needs to know WHY she is sacrificing in the short term, but she also needs to feel the pain of what will happen if she doesn't change… and feel the joy of success when she sticks to the plan. It's much more visceral than just, "I better start watching my spending."

4. What if your values come in conflict?

Welcome to life! This is actually where it gets fun. Life would be really boring if we could always choose quickly and easily. In fact, most of life is spent in the gray area.

If there's one thing I know for sure, it's that you're ALWAYS going to have to make some tough choices. Your son's field trip is the same time you have a big work presentation. Your best friend calls in crisis mode the same time you were going to work on your novel. It goes on and on. We rarely get cut-and-dried choices; there's usually an element of having to disappoint someone involved in our biggest choices.

FOUND

Here are some tips for you to follow:

Think in terms of seasons. "To everything there is a season," says the Bible (and Peter, Paul, and Mary). It's so true – your kids may need you more now, and this time with them will never come again. You may choose to prioritize them over other activities now because it's their last year at home, or because you'll never get this chance again. Just know WHY you are doing it, and make sure you're not using it as an easy excuse.

This coming year is my son's senior year in high school. You better believe I'm going to be at every home baseball game, every senior mom event, and every parent activity – whether he wants me there or not! This is the last chance I have to make these choices. Next year, things will be different. With one kid off at school, I'll have more time on my own. That's when I'll start training to run a marathon. Maybe.

Rotate. When my kids were younger I had them take turns being "kid for the day." They got to choose the TV show, where they wanted to sit in the car, and whether we'd have spaghetti or chicken for dinner. It cut down on a huge amount of arguments and sibling squabbles and saved my sanity – or at least part of it.

You can use this same approach with your values. If you choose to work out today instead of watching TV with your family, next week put family first a time or two. If you're going on a girls' weekend next week, opt to hang out with the kids this weekend. Something may be in the highest slot for your priorities, but it doesn't mean you don't do anything else.

Benjamin Franklin was a great rotator. He had 13 virtues about which he wrote in his autobiography. He decided to focus on each virtue for one week at a time, and then move on to the next. That would mean each virtue would be front and center once a quarter over the course of a whole year. If it worked for him, it's probably worth trying for us!

Layer activities. As a veteran multi-tasker, I love this one! Multi-tasking gets a bad rap. Nearly everywhere online you can read about how multi-tasking is an absolutely horrible idea and causes lower productivity and performance. But I think that just means people aren't doing it right.

I like to "layer" activities. There are some activities that require my presence but not my attention (baseball games, anyone?) or my attention but not my actual presence (conference calls, for instance). I can combine these two types of activities so my body is in one place, but my mind is elsewhere. I can tune back in when Ben is up to bat or our team is in the field.

There are even more activities that can be shared amongst two or more priorities. If you want to spend time with your kids AND get in shape, go for a run with your kids riding their bikes next to you. If you value creativity AND friendship, ask your best friend to take an art class with you. There are tons of ways to combine two or more of your values.

5. **What if you don't know what's important?**

Feeling like you have no idea what's important is very common, particularly if you've been putting yourself last for a long time. That's why I assign my coaching clients the homework of giving themselves a "little joy" each and every day.

FOUND

A little joy is anything that makes your heart sing. When we start trying to figure out what we want, it's natural that we think of the big stuff – what is our life's work, where do we want to live, who do we want to be in a relationship with. But just as you have to figure out algebra before you can move on to trigonometry, you need to figure out the little stuff before the big stuff becomes clear.

What makes you smile? A new set of colored pencils? Reading a murder mystery? Getting your nails done? Buying a new cookbook? Each of these is a clue to your heart and soul. Pay attention. Write them down. Make lists. Take photos. Start a Pinterest board or a joy journal. You'll begin to see themes and commonalities.

Also pay attention to when you feel that pit-of-the-stomach ache. It's a sure sign that you've done something out of key with your values. Again, make note of these clenching-of-the-loins feelings. When did they occur? Who were you with? What had you just agreed to? Where were you? Figure out what you DON'T want and you'll naturally start moving towards what you DO want.

One other suggestion: Create. We have become such a culture of consumers, whether it's sitting back and letting someone else entertain us, or pinning someone else's creative work on Pinterest. It's time for you to throw some back into the pot by making instead of just merely consuming. Paint a picture. Do a five-minute sketch a day. Write bad poetry. Knit a sock. Cook a meal without a recipe. There are a million and one ways to exercise your creativity, and each one is a bread crumb back to your soul.

6. What if I do all this work and then decide it's not worth it?

I can almost guarantee you that getting to know yourself and living a life defined by your terms is totally worth the effort and pain, but I know you won't believe me until you've done it yourself. So I'll tell you two things:

One, I've never had a client go through this process and wish that she hadn't. Instead, it's the opposite: I hear statements like, "This is life-changing! Why didn't I do this ten (or twenty, or thirty) years ago!" And, "Thank you, thank you, thank you. This was the most important thing I've done for myself." So chances are very good that a few months from now, you'll be saying the same thing!

Two, you can always go back. If you decide it wasn't worth the effort and you liked your life better before you started stripping off all the old wallpaper, you can return right back to where you were. You can pull out those old routines, habits, obligations and relationships, and jump right back in. But you won't want to.

Trust me, you've got nothing to lose and everything to gain. Give it a shot.

7. This sounds like a lot of work!

It can be. But it truly is the most important work you can do to live a full life, being who you were created to be. And it can be really fun, too! Try to embark on it with a sense of play and fun, rather than seeing it as another chore to undertake. People who have tackled this will tell you that their lives have literally changed for the better and they've dropped

FOUND

so much of what held them back. They feel like butterflies emerging from a cocoon!

Even if I could, I wouldn't wave a magic wand to grant you the wish of a fully authentic life. So many lessons need to be learned first-hand, going through the process, making the tough decisions, dealing with the gray areas.

If you want to soar, you have to put in the effort. But it will be worth it, and I'm here to help you.

CHAPTER 13

YOUR ACTION PLAN

I invite you to use this action plan as a way to put these suggestions and ideas to work for you. It's not enough to just read about it – you have to DO IT. Sometimes we have no idea where we're going until we take that first step, and then the next, and then the next. But moving forward requires shifting the car out of "park" and into "drive" and putting your foot on the gas. It doesn't have to take a ton of time; in fact, just 15 minutes a day of reflecting on that day's activities and goals is enough to get you moving in the right direction.

1. Go through a values assessment (see resource section for examples). This will give you a good snapshot of what is important to you right now. Then you can compare where you are spending your time now, now in relationto the things you've declared as most important. Look for disconnects.

2. Download the free Authenticity Worksheets available from my website at http://www.lainehmann.com/freeauthenticityworksheets. Fill them out!

3. Set aside 15 minutes per day for the next 21 days to fill out a daily accountability sheet (get it here: http://www.lainehmann.com/freeauthenticityworksheets). Also work through the questions and

exercises proposed in the previous sections. Make note of any "AHA!" moments and surprises, or when you feel upset or angry. High emotion is a great sign that you've tapped into an area that needs further examination. (It's a great idea to have a journal, notebook, or computer file specifically for this purpose. Writing down your notes, thoughts, and goals will make them even more concrete.)

4. Watch or read additional books and talks on the topic of authenticity (see the resources section). Living an authentic life is an ongoing process. You never "get there," though you will get closer and closer. The goal is not perfection, but refinement and progress. You can do this!

5. Join a coaching program for additional support. We'd love to have you! Visit my website at www.lainehmann.com/coaching for more information on current programs.

RESOURCES

Values Assessment: http://www.career-test.biz/values_assessment.htm
Another Values Assessment: http://www.mindtools.com/pages/article/newTED_85.htm

Daring Greatly by Brene Brown
http://www.lainehmann.com/daring

Brene Brown's "The Power of Vulnerability" TED talk:
https://youtu.be/iCvmsMzlF7o

Start with Why by Simon Sinek
http://www.lainehmann.com/why

Simon Sinek's "Start with Why" TED talk:
https://youtu.be/sioZd3AxmnE

Your Free Authenticity Worksheets: http://www.lainehmann.com/freeauthenticityworksheets

YOUR INVITATION

❖

The process of becoming yourself is unbelievably rewarding, exciting, and darned hard. We have this vision that once we get our "stuff" straightened out, everything else in our lives will fall into place. Unfortunately, it's not so. In fact, the stronger our own light shines, the more likely it is that others get scared, intimidated, or envious of our progress. You know how your girlfriends are all in favor of your losing 20 lbs. and becoming a hottie – that is, until you start getting all the attention when you go out on Friday night. Then you become a target for their criticism of how you're getting too big for your britches (or becoming something that rhymes with "britches!").

People don't like it when we change. It requires them to examine their own bad habits and excuses, and many people aren't prepared for that level of self-examination. They'd rather you went along as you always had, not making waves, not causing any issues.

So what do you do when you long to be who you are, no apologies, but the world around you is bound and determined to keep you stuck in the same old box?

You keep forging forward, and you find company for the journey.

After spending the last few years working with women who are learning to live their lives loud, I have seen the power of community. It's nearly impossible to keep true to yourself without a group of people you can lean on when times get tough. Why do you think Weight Watchers is so successful? I mean, their chocolate snack cakes aren't that magical. But what is magical is the feeling of camaraderie and support when you are meeting regularly with a group of people who are right there in the trenches with you. Your chances of continuing to live your authentic life will increase exponentially if you have a support structure.

That's the very reason I created my group coaching program, Living Life Loud. This program provides the structure and support needed to keep true to yourself, even when times get tough. If you'd like to find out more about it – and to receive a special offer for my readers – please visit http://www.lainehmann.com/Foundbookoffer.

I'd absolutely love to work with you!

ABOUT THE AUTHOR

❖

After building my online business to six figures in only 18 months, I began coaching other women to do the same. But through my business coaching I discovered that knowing WHAT to do was only part of the battle; the bigger challenge was helping my clients believe that they COULD have the business – and the life – of their dreams. While I still do a bit of business coaching, I've shifted my focus to helping women find their unique voice amidst the cacophony of family, friends, societal demands, and expectations.

I offer a variety of coaching programs, from monthly group coaching to one-on-one sessions, through which I help women live their lives LOUD, sharing their gifts and talents with the world, and holding nothing back!

With degrees from Stanford University and Syracuse University, and decades in the professional and entrepreneurial world, I love finding innovative and unexpected solutions to life's challenges and problems. My gift is sorting through the overwhelm of ing information, ideas, expectations, and noise to find the simple path that leads back to YOU.

You can find out more about me and my programs at www.lainehmann.com.

Made in the USA
Columbia, SC
22 September 2021